New York Giants Football Quiz Book

500 Questions On Big Blue

Chris Bradshaw

Copyright © 2018 Chris Bradshaw

All rights reserved.

ISBN: 1984936476
ISBN-13: 978-1984936479

Front cover image created by headfuzz by grimboid. Check out his collection of sport, movie, music and TV posters at

https://www.etsy.com/shop/headfuzzbygrimboid

Introduction

Think you know about the New York Giants? Put your knowledge to the test with this selection of quizzes on all things Big Blue.

The book covers the whole history of the franchise from the early days at the Polo Grounds through to the glorious World Championship teams of Bill Parcells and Tom Coughlin and beyond.

The biggest names in Giants history are present and correct so look out for questions on Lawrence Taylor, Phil Simms, Eli Manning, Odell Beckham Jr., Harry Carson and many, many more.

There are 500 questions in all covering running backs and receivers, coaches and quarterbacks, pass rushers and punters and much else besides.

Each quiz contains a selection of 20 questions and is either a mixed bag of pot luck testers or is centered on a specific category such as quarterbacks or defense.

There are easy, medium and hard questions offering something for New York novices as well as professors of Giants history.

You'll find the answers to each quiz below the bottom of the following quiz. For example, the answers to Quiz 1: Pot Luck, are underneath Quiz 2: Quarterbacks. The only exception is Quiz 25: Numbers Game. The answers to these can be found under the Quiz 1 questions.

Statistics relate to the regular season only unless otherwise stated and are accurate to the end of the 2017 season.

We hope you enjoy the New York Giants Football Quiz Book.

About the Author

Chris Bradshaw (no relation to Ahmad) has written 16 quiz books including titles for Britain's biggest selling daily newspaper, The Sun, and The Times (of London). In addition to the NFL, he has written extensively on soccer, cricket, darts and poker.

He lives in Birmingham, England and has been following the NFL for over 30 years.

Acknowledgements

Many thanks to Ken and Veronica Bradshaw, Heidi Grant, Steph, James, Ben and Will Roe and Graham Nash.

CONTENTS

1	Pot Luck	8
2	Quarterbacks	10
3	Pot Luck	12
4	Running Backs	14
5	Pot Luck	16
6	Receivers	18
7	Pot Luck	20
8	Defense	22
9	Pot Luck	24
10	Special Teams	26
11	Pot Luck	28
12	1986 World Champions	30
13	Pot Luck	32
14	1990 World Champions	34
15	Pot Luck	36
16	2007 World Champions	38

17	Pot Luck	40
18	2011 World Champions	42
19	Pot Luck	44
20	Eli Manning	46
21	Pot Luck	48
22	History	50
23	Pot Luck	52
24	Anagrams	54
25	Numbers Game	56

Quiz 1: Pot Luck

1. Who was appointed the 18th head coach of the Giants in January 2018?

2. Which defensive superstar played in 216 games for the Giants between 1993 and 2007?

3. Who famously said, 'I'm going to Disney World' after his stellar performance in Super Bowl XXI?

4. What number jersey did quarterback Phil Simms wear?

5. What was the fishy nickname of legendary Giants coach Bill Parcells?

6. 'Rambo' was the nickname of which tough Giants tight end?

7. Which Giants receiver was noted for his salsa-dance touchdown celebrations?

8. In what year did the Giants move into MetLife Stadium?

9. Which team did the Giants defeat 31-18 in the first regular season game staged at MetLife Stadium?

10. What color jerseys did the Giants wear while winning Super Bowl XLV?

11. Throughout their entire history do the Giants have an overall winning or losing record?

12. Between 1970 and 2017, three Giants head coaches took the team to the playoffs in their first season. Which three?

13. True or false – The 2007 Giants were the first NFC wild card team to win a Super Bowl?

14. Which team did the Giants defeat in the game nicknamed 'Ice Bowl 2'?

15. Which alliteratively-named receiver's 65 catches in 2016 were the third most by a rookie in team history?

16. In 2001, which Giants quarterback set the NFL record for the most fumbles in a season with 23?

17. In 1972, the Giants scored a team record 62 points against which divisional foe?

18. With which pick of the 2014 NFL Draft did the Giants select receiver Odell Beckham Jr?

19. How many home games did the Giants win during their 2007 World Championship season? a) three b) four c) five

20. Between 2004 and 2017 Eli Manning started how many straight games? a) 200 b) 210 c) 220

Quiz 25: Answers

1. #20 2. #13 3. #80 4. #27 5. #3 6. #12 7. #31 8. #52 9. #5 10. #76 11. #9 12. #21 13. #89 14. #91 15. #17 16. #58 17. #72 18. #44 19. #15 20. #81

Quiz 2: Quarterbacks

1. Who is the all-time franchise leader in passing yards?

2. Which quarterback did the Giants trade to acquire the services of Eli Manning?

3. Which team formed the other half of that famous 2004 trade?

4. Which third round draft pick steered the Giants to victory in Super Bowl XXV?

5. Who made more playoff appearances for the Giants – Phil Simms or Eli Manning?

6. In a January 2001 game against the Vikings, who became the first Giants quarterback to throw five touchdown passes in a single playoff contest?

7. Who won more games as a starting quarterback with the Giants – Dave Brown or Danny Kanell?

8. Eli Manning holds the record for the most 300-yard passing games in franchise history. Who is second on that list?

9. Who holds the franchise record for the most passing yards in a single game with 513?

10. Which Hall of Fame quarterback threw 103 touchdown passes during a five-season spell in New York between 1967 and 1971?

11. Who was the last Giants quarterback to lead the NFC in passing yards?

12. Which former number one overall pick had two spells with the Giants in 2008 and 2009 and then again in 2011 and 2012?

13. Eli Manning is one of only two Giants to attempt over 550 passes in a single regular season. Who is the other?

14. Which California quarterback did the Giants select in the third round of the 2017 NFL Draft?

15. Which Hall of Famer enjoyed a 5-4 record in his single season with the Giants in 2004?

16. Who are the two Giants to have completed 40 passes in a single regular season game?

17. Eli Manning threw six touchdown passes in a November 2015 game against which NFC South team?

18. In a 2017 game against the Raiders, who became the first quarterback not named Eli Manning to start for the Giants in 13 years?

19. How many regular season touchdown passes did Phil Simms throw for the Giants? a) 198 b) 199 c) 200

20. Eli Manning threw how many passes during a December 2016 game against Philadelphia a) 59 b) 61 c) 63

Quiz 1: Answers

1. Pat Shurmur 2. Michael Strahan 3. Phil Simms 4. #11 5. Big Tuna 6. Mark Bavaro 7. Victor Cruz 8. 2010 9. Carolina 10. White 11. Winning 12. Dan Reeves, Jim Fassel and Ben McAdoo 13. True 14. Green Bay 15. Sterling Shepard 16. Kerry Collins 17. Philadelphia 18. 12th 19. a) Three 20. b) 210

11

Quiz 3: Pot Luck

1. Linebacker Lawrence Taylor wore what number jersey?

2. Eli Manning played college ball at which southern school?

3. Which quarterback spent 15 years with the Giants between 1979 and 1993?

4. Who was the first Giant to lead the league in single-season sacks more than once?

5. 'Snacks' is the nickname of which Giants defensive lineman?

6. Who was the first Giant to appear on the cover of the Madden video game?

7. The Giants played their second regular season game in London in October 2016 against which team?

8. What was the score in that game?

9. Which stadium, better known as a rugby union venue, hosted that London game?

10. True or false – The Giants were the only team from the NFC to appear in the Super Bowl more than once in the 2000s?

11. The Giants were on the wrong end of a 52-49 shoot out to which team in November 2015?

12. Which four-time Pro Bowl guard, who spent his entire career with the Giants, is the son-in-law of former head coach Tom Coughlin?

13. Which receiver returned a punt for a touchdown as time expired to give Philadelphia a shock 38-31 win over the Giants in December 2010?

14. The Giants played their home games in the 1975 season at which baseball park?

15. Do the Giants have a winning or losing record in Sunday Night Football games?

16. Which former Giant wrote the 2015 bestseller 'Wake Up Happy: The Dream Big, Win Big Guide to Transforming Your Life'?

17. In 2002, who set the record for the most catches by a rookie tight end in team history with 74?

18. Which receiver holds the record for the most receiving touchdowns in franchise history?

19. In what year did the Giants revert to having an NY rather than Giants logo on their helmets? a) 1980 b) 1990 c) 2000

20. The 2007 Giants set an NFL record after winning how many straight games away from home? a) 9 b) 10 c) 11

Quiz 2: Answers

1. Eli Manning 2. Philip Rivers 3. San Diego Chargers 4. Jeff Hostetler 5. Eli Manning 6. Kerry Collins 7. Dave Brown 8. Phil Simms 9. Phil Simms 10. Fran Tarkenton 11. Phil Simms 12. David Carr 13. Kerry Collins 14. Davis Webb 15. Kurt Warner 16. Eli Manning and Phil Simms 17. New Orleans 18. Geno Smith 19. b) 199 20. c) 63

Quiz 4: Running Backs

1. Who is the Giants' all-time leading rusher?

2. The longest rush in franchise history was a 95-yard scamper by Tiki Barber on New Year's Eve 2005 against which team?

3. Which running back was named the MVP of Super Bowl XXV after rushing for 102 yards?

4. The Giants used their 2012 first round draft pick to select which running back?

5. Which running back rushed for over 1,000 yards in both 2010 and 2012?

6. Which running back holds the record for the most rushing touchdowns in franchise history with 60?

7. In 2008, Brandon Jacobs was one of two Giants running backs to enjoy a 1,000-yard season. Who was the other?

8. Who holds the franchise record for the most rushing yards and attempts in postseason games?

9. With 6,897 yards between 1990 and 1997, who is second on the franchise all-time rushing list?

10. The Giants rushed for over 300 yards in a 2008 game against which NFC South team?

11. In December 2006, Tiki Barber rushed for a franchise record 234 yards against which division rival?

12. The Giants used the 12th overall pick of the 2000 NFL Draft to select which Wisconsin running back?

13. Which Giants running back was named the PFWA NFL Comeback Player of the Year for 1989?

14. True or false – In 1999, Joe Montgomery led the team in rushing despite amassing just 348 yards?

15. Which running back holds the franchise record for scoring the most touchdowns in a season with 21?

16. Of Giants backs with over 500 attempts, who has the best yards per carry average?

17. In a 1983 game against the Eagles, which former Michigan star set a then NFL record with 43 rushing attempts?

18. In 2004, which Giants running back scored a touchdown in seven straight games?

19. Tiki Barber enjoyed how many 100-yard rushing games with the Giants? a) 19 b) 29 c) 39

20. Rodney Hampton tied a franchise record after scoring four touchdowns in a 1995 game against which NFC team? a) Atlanta b) New Orleans c) Tampa Bay

Quiz 3: Answers

1. #56 2. Mississippi 3. Phil Simms 4. Michael Strahan 5. Damon Harrison 6. Odell Beckham Jr. 7. St Louis Rams 8. Giants 17-10 Rams 9. Twickenham 10. True 11. New Orleans 12. Chris Snee 13. DeSean Jackson 14. Shea Stadium 15. Losing 16. Michael Strahan 17. Jeremy Shockey 18. Amani Toomer 19. c) 2000 20. c) 11

Quiz 5: Pot Luck

1. Since the 1970 merger, which head coach has guided the Giants to the most regular season wins?

2. The Giants have defeated which opponent the most times in team history?

3. What color jerseys did the Giants wear while winning Super Bowl XXI?

4. What was the nickname of the linebacking quartet made up of Brad Van Pelt, Lawrence Taylor, Harry Carson and Brian Kelley?

5. Which linebacker won two Super Bowl rings with the 1986 and 1990 Giants then three more as an assistant coach with New England?

6. Between 1925 and 1955 the Giants played home games at which famous venue?

7. Who won more games as Giants head coach – Jim Fassel or Dan Reeves?

8. True or false – Between 1970 and 2017 the Giants never lost an NFC Championship Game?

9. Who are the two Giants quarterbacks with over 4,000 passing yards in a single season?

10. True or false – No Giants running back rushed for over 1,000 yards in a season between 2013 and 2017?

11. Whose 207 appearances between 1989 and 2001 are the most by a Giants tight end?

12. In a 1933 game against Boston, Harry Newman became the first Giants player to do what?

13. Who is the only Giant to lead the NFL in single-season touchdowns?

14. True or false – In a 1952 game against Pittsburgh the Giants had seven passes intercepted?

15. Is the field at MetLife Stadium made up of grass or artificial turf?

16. What name is missing from this list – Perkins, Parcells, ????, Reeves?

17. @TheHumble_21 is the Twitter handle of which Giants defensive star?

18. The Giants sent a conditional draft pick to which team to acquire the services of punter Brad Wing?

19. How many games did the Giants win in Tom Coughlin's first season as head coach of the Giants? a) five b) six c) seven

20. What is the official seating capacity of MetLife Stadium? a) 80,200 b) 82,500 c) 85,200

Quiz 4: Answers

1. Tiki Barber 2. Oakland 3. Ottis 'OJ' Anderson 4. David Wilson 5. Ahmad Bradshaw 6. Brandon Jacobs 7. Derrick Ward 8. Joe Morris 9. Rodney Hampton 10. Carolina 11. Washington 12. Ron Dayne 13. Ottis 'OJ' Anderson 14. True 15. Joe Morris 16. Tiki Barber 17. Butch Woolfolk 18. Tiki Barber 19. c) 39 20. b) New Orleans

Quiz 6: Receivers

1. With 668 catches, who is the Giants' all-time leading receiver?

2. In 2009, who became the first receiver in franchise history with over 100 catches in a season?

3. Who set the team record for the most receiving yards in a season with 1,536 in 2011?

4. Who caught the touchdown pass that sealed victory for the Giants in the closing stages of Super Bowl XLII?

5. With 371 catches, who holds the franchise record for the most receptions by a tight end?

6. Which rookie tight end led the team in receptions during the ill-fated 2017 season?

7. Which receiver's 99-yard catch against the Jets on Christmas Eve 2011 is the longest in franchise history?

8. Who holds the record for the most catches by a running back in franchise history?

9. Who is the only Giants tight end to enjoy a 1,000-yard receiving season?

10. With 1,214 and 1,025 yards respectively, who led the team in receiving yards in 2005 and 2007?

11. In 2015, Odell Beckham Jr. tied the team record for the most touchdown receptions in a season with how many?

12. Who caught 10 passes for 109 yards and a touchdown in Super Bowl XLVI?

13. In 2006, who became the first Giants receiver to score a hat-trick of touchdowns in a single playoff game?

14. Odell Beckham Jr. amassed 222 receiving yards in a 2016 game against which AFC North team?

15. Which receiver, who later won two Super Bowl rings with Denver, led the Giants in receiving in 1992?

16. Which alliteratively-named receiver led the team in receptions in 1995, 1996, 1997 and 1998?

17. Which receiver's 368 catches between 1997 and 2004 are good for fifth place on the all-time franchise record list?

18. Which Giants receiver led the NFC in receptions in 1983?

19. Which Giant holds the record for the best yards per catch average in NFL history (min. 200 catches)? c) Bart Jones b) Homer Jones c) Montgomery Jones

20. Between 1998 and 2004 Amani Toomer caught passes in how many consecutive games? a) 88 b) 93 c) 98

Quiz 5: Answers

1. Tom Coughlin 2. Washington 3. Blue 4. The Crunch Bunch 5. Pepper Johnson 6. The Polo Grounds 7. Jim Fassel 8. True 9. Eli Manning and Kerry Collins 10. True 11. Howard Cross 12. Rush for 100 yards in a game 13. Joe Morris 14. True 15. Artificial turf 16. Handley 17. Landon Collins 18. Pittsburgh 19. b) Six 20. b) 82,500

Quiz 7: Pot Luck

1. Who holds the record for the most all-purpose yards in franchise history?

2. Since its foundation, the Giants franchise has been owned or part owned by one family. Which one?

3. Which back led the team in rushing for six straight years between 1991 and 1996?

4. What number jersey was worn by former Giants great Frank Gifford?

5. Which former Denver head coach took charge in New York in 1993?

6. Which Giants quarterback threw 76 passes in the playoffs, none of which were picked off?

7. Who holds the team record for the most Pro Bowl appearances with 10?

8. Which division rival did the Giants face in their first ever regular season game at Giants Stadium?

9. True or false – No Giants running back has led the NFL in rushing since the 1950s?

10. Do the Giants have an overall winning or losing record in overtime games?

11. In 2012, which running back set the franchise record for the most all-purpose yards in a game after racking up 327 against the Saints?

12. True of false – Eli Manning was the first quarterback in NFL history to lose 100 games with the same team?

20

13. In 2015, Odell Beckham Jr. received a one-game suspension after repeatedly clashing with which Carolina defensive back?

14. True or false – In the 1950s the Giants coaching staff included both Vince Lombardi and Tom Landry?

15. The Giants have used more first round draft picks to select players in which position than any other?

16. Which former Giants defensive coordinator later won NFC and AFC Championship titles but not a Super Bowl as a head coach?

17. Who holds the franchise record for throwing the most career interceptions?

18. In 2014, who tied the franchise record for the most touchdowns by a Giants rookie with 12?

19. What is former star offensive lineman Jumbo Elliott's real first name? a) John b) Paul c) George

20. How many games did the Giants win in Bill Parcells' first season as head coach? a) three b) four c) five

Quiz 6: Answers

1. Amani Toomer 2. Steve Smith 3. Victor Cruz 4. Plaxico Burress 5. Jeremy Shockey 6. Evan Engram 7. Victor Cruz 8. Tiki Barber 9. Mark Bavaro 10. Plaxico Burress 11. 13 12. Hakeem Nicks 13. Amani Toomer 14. Baltimore 15. Ed McCaffrey 16. Chris Calloway 17. Ike Hilliard 18. Earnest Gray 19. b) Homer Jones 20. c) 98

Quiz 8: Defense

1. Who is the Giants' all-time leader in sacks?

2. Which Giant was named the AP NFL MVP for the 1986 season?

3. Which linebacker, who went to the Pro Bowl nine times between 1978 and 1987, was elected into the Pro Football Hall of Fame in 2006?

4. Who led the team in sacks in 2011, 2012, 2014 and 2017?

5. Who picked off eight passes in 2012, returning them for a franchise record 307 yards?

6. Who sacked John Elway to score a safety in Super Bowl XXI?

7. Who holds the franchise record for the most sacks in a single game?

8. How many sacks did he record to set that record?

9. Which Ohio State cornerback did the Giants select with the 10th pick of the 2016 NFL Draft?

10. Which former Jets defensive tackle won First-Team All-Pro honors with the Giants after a stellar 2016 season?

11. Which cornerback, who played for the Giants between 1994 and 2002, holds the team record for the most interceptions in playoff games?

12. True or false – In 2003, the Giants defense intercepted just 10 passes?

13. With which pick of the 1981 NFL Draft did the Giants select Lawrence Taylor?

14. Defensive lineman Osi Umenyiora was born in which European capital city?

15. Whose 79.5 sacks between 1983 and 1993 are good enough for third place on the team's all-time list?

16. Which long-serving defensive tackle holds the record for the longest fumble return in team history after taking one back 87 yards against the Chiefs in 1995?

17. Which Hall of Fame coach intercepted a pass in seven straight games while playing with the Giants in the early 1950s?

18. Which linebacker returned an interception 97 yards for a touchdown against the Lions in November 1982?

19. Who holds the franchise record for the most sacks in a single season? a) Jason Pierre Paul b) Michael Strahan c) Lawrence Taylor

20. How many sacks did he record in that record-breaking season? a) 20.5 b) 21.5 c) 22.5

Quiz 7: Answers

1. Tiki Barber 2. The Mara Family 3. Rodney Hampton 4. #16 5. Dan Reeves 6. Jeff Hostetler 7. Lawrence Taylor 8. Dallas 9. True 10. Winning 11. David Wilson 12. True 13. Josh Norman 14. True 15. Running back 16. John Fox 17. Eli Manning 18. Odell Beckham Jr. 19. a) John 20. a) Three

Quiz 9: Pot Luck

1. Which head coach was fired after 13 games of the 2017 regular season?

2. Who holds the record for the most fumbles in franchise history?

3. The Giants played their final home game at which famous venue on 23 September 1973?

4. Who were the two starters on the Super Bowl XLII team whose first name and surname started with the same letter? (clue – one was a tight end, the other an O-lineman)

5. Quarterback Kerry Collins joined the Giants in 1999 after being released by which team?

6. What is the highest number of regular season games that the Giants have won in a single season?

7. 'Over The Edge' was the subtitle of the autobiography of which former Giants star?

8. The Giants have lost more regular season games against which opponent than any other?

9. Which alliteratively-named wide receiver caught a 92-yard touchdown pass against Washington in January 2011?

10. Who was the last Giant before Odell Beckham Jr. to make it to the Pro Bowl in each of his first three seasons in the NFL?

11. Which defensive lineman, who played between 1975 and 1988, is one of only four Giants to have played in over 200 regular season games?

12. Which quarterback, who won just one of his nine starts with the Giants between 1971 and 1973, has the same name as an all-time great baseball pitcher?

13. True or false – In 2011, Eli Manning set the NFL record for throwing the most fourth quarter touchdown passes in a single season with 15?

14. Which defensive lineman set a franchise record after recovering five fumbles during the 2010 regular season?

15. The first regular season game broadcast live on ESPN was a 1987 contest between the Giants and which AFC rival?

16. How many postseason games did the Giants play throughout the whole of the 1970s?

17. What color jerseys did the Giants wear in Super Bowl XLII?

18. True or false – The Giants were the first NFL team to retire a jersey number?

19. How many regular season games did the Giants win during Bill Parcells' eight-year spell as head coach? a) 67 b) 77 c) 87

20. What is the most points allowed by the Giants in a single game? a) 52 b) 62 c) 72

Quiz 8: Answers

1. Michael Strahan 2. Lawrence Taylor 3. Harry Carson 4. Jason Pierre-Paul 5. Stevie Brown 6. George Martin 7. Osi Umenyiora 8. Six 9. Eli Apple 10. Damon Harrison 11. Jason Sehorn 12. True 13. Second 14. London 15. Leonard Marshall 16. Keith Hamilton 17. Tom Landry 18. Lawrence Taylor 19. b) Michael Strahan 20. c) 22.5

Quiz 10: Special Teams

1. With 646 points between 1966 and 1974 which kicker is the Giants' all-time leading point scorer?

2. Who was the kicker on the Super Bowl XLII and XLVI-winning teams?

3. Whose 100-yard kickoff return against the Cowboys in October 2015 tied the franchise record?

4. Which legendary Giants receiver set the record for the longest punt return in team history after taking one back for an 87-yard touchdown against the Bills in September 1996?

5. Which kicker converted 123 fields goals and 157 extra points in a Giants career that ran from 1993 through to 2000?

6. Which punter was named a First-Team All-Pro in 1986, 1989 and 1990?

7. True or false – Former kicker Lawrence Tynes was born in Ireland?

8. Which much-traveled 44-year-old kicker went 35-38 on field goal attempts for the Giants during the 2008 season?

9. Whose 97-yard kickoff return touchdown was the only highlight of the Giants' Super Bowl XXXV loss to Baltimore?

10. Which kicker converted a team playoff record five field goals to send the Giants to Super Bowl XXV?

11. Which star running back returned a punt 85 yards for a touchdown against Dallas in October 1999?

12. In 2005, who became the first Giant to lead the NFL in most points by a kicker since the 1950s?

13. What is the longest successful field goal in franchise history?

14. Who converted that record-breaking distance twice during the 1983 season?

15. In 2011, which Giant became the first player in NFL history to kick two game-winning overtime field goals in playoff games?

16. Who was the kicker on the Super Bowl XXI roster?

17. Who holds the franchise record for converting the most field goals in a row after booting 29 straight in 2014 and 2015?

18. Which receiver returned 213 punts between 1984 and 1988, the second most in franchise history, despite having a longest return of just 37 yards?

19. Rodney Williams set the record for the longest punt in team history in Denver in 2001. How long was it? a) 70 yards b) 80 yards c) 90 yards

20. What is the most points scored by a Giants kicker in a single season? a) 140 b) 144 c) 148

Quiz 9: Answers

1. Ben McAdoo 2. Eli Manning 3. Yankee Stadium 4. Michael Matthews and David Diehl 5. New Orleans 6. 14 games 7. Lawrence Taylor 8. Philadelphia 9. Mario Manningham 10. Lawrence Taylor 11. George Martin 12. Randy Johnson 13. True 14. Justin Tuck 15. New England 16. None 17. White 18. True 19. b) 77 20. c) 72

Quiz 11: Pot Luck

1. In which round of the 1997 NFL Draft did the Giants select star running back Tiki Barber?

2. Which Giant has been named a First-Team All-Pro more times than any other player?

3. Which broadcaster does the play-by-play commentary for the Giants Radio Network?

4. Which former Giants defensive great is the co-commentator on Giants radio broadcasts?

5. Which Giant was named the AP NFL Offensive Rookie of the Year in 2014?

6. Prior to Evan Engram, whose was the last tight end selected by the Giants in the first round of the NFL Draft?

7. To the nearest thousand, the MetLife Stadium parking lot has spaces for how many cars?

8. Which former Giant has made TV and movie appearances in 'The Sopranos', 'The Waterboy' and 'Shaft 2000'?

9. True or false – In a 1950 game against Baltimore the Giants amassed 423 rushing yards?

10. Who are the three Giants head coaches to win the AP NFL Coach of the Year Award in the Super Bowl era?

11. Which long-time Giant co-wrote a children's book called 'Family Huddle' with his father and brother?

12. Which commentator, best known for his partnership with John Madden, played for the Giants from 1958 until 1961?

13. What number jersey did legendary linebacker Harry Carson wear?

14. Who was the next Giant after Lawrence Taylor to be voted to the Pro Bowl in each of his first two seasons in the league?

15. What do the Giants have in common with the Buffalo Bills, Chicago Bears, Green Bay Packers, Pittsburgh Steelers and Cleveland Browns?

16. True or false – Despite being voted to numerous Pro Bowls, linebacker Harry Carson was never named a First-Team All-Pro?

17. Which franchise was in the same division as the Giants until 2001 before moving to the NFC West?

18. Up to the start of the 2018 season the Giants had a 100% playoff record against which three NFC opponents?

19. Which linebacker set a then team record after recording 4.5 sacks in a 1991 game against the Bucs? a) Carl Banks b) Pepper Johnson c) Lawrence Taylor

20. What was the highest number of touchdown passes thrown by Eli Manning in a single regular season? a) 33 b) 35 c) 37

Quiz 10: Answers

1. Pete Gogolak 2. Lawrence Tynes 3. Dwayne Harris 4. Amani Toomer 5. Brad Daluiso 6. Sean Landeta 7. False – He was born in Scotland 8. John Carney 9. Ron Dixon 10. Matt Bahr 11. Tiki Barber 12. Jay Feely 13. 56 yards 14. Ali Haji-Sheikh 15. Lawrence Tynes 16. Raul Allegre 17. Josh Brown 18. Phil McConkey 19. c) 90 yards 20. c) 148

Quiz 12: 1986 World Champions

1. Which team did the Giants defeat in Super Bowl XXI?

2. What was the final score in the game?

3. Which famous stadium hosted Super Bowl XXI?

4. Who was named the game's Most Valuable Player?

5. Which two Giants scored rushing touchdowns in Super Bowl XXI?

6. Which three receivers caught touchdown passes in the game?

7. Which head coach steered the Giants to their maiden Super Bowl victory?

8. With 1,516 yards, who was New York's top rusher in 1986?

9. The Giants' defensive coordinator from 1986 went on to have a stellar head coaching career. Who was he?

10. What was the team's regular season record in 1986?

11. Who were the only teams to defeat the Giants during the 1986 season?

12. The Giants reached Super Bowl XXI after beating which division rival in the NFC Championship game?

13. The Giants routed which team 49-3 in the Divisional round playoff?

14. True or false – Phil Simms completed just nine passes in that 49-3 playoff victory?

15. With 66 catches for 1,001 yards, who was New York's leading receiver in 1986?

16. What was the nickname of the legendary defense that dominated throughout 1986?

17. The Giants closed out the 1986 regular season by putting 55 points on which NFC rival?

18. Which future head coach with the Browns and Chiefs was the Giants' special teams coordinator in 1986?

19. How many points did the Giants score in the second half of Super Bowl XXI? a) 17 b) 24 c) 30

20. Lawrence Taylor was one of two Giants to record double-digit sacks in 1986. Who was the other? a) Jim Burt b) Harry Carson c) Leonard Marshall

Quiz 11: Answers

1. Second 2. Lawrence Taylor 3. Bob Papa 4. Carl Banks 5. Odell Beckham Jr. 6. Jeremy Shockey 7. 28,000 8. Lawrence Taylor 9. True 10. Bill Parcells, Dan Reeves and Jim Fassel 11. Eli Manning 12. Pat Summerall 13. #53 14. Jeremy Shockey 15. They don't have cheerleaders 16. True 17. The Cardinals 18. Atlanta, Dallas and Tampa Bay 19. b) Pepper Johnson 20. b) 35

Quiz 13: Pot Luck

1. In what year was the Giants franchise founded?

2. Before being named the head coach of the Giants Pat Shurmur was the offensive coordinator at which NFC team?

3. Do the Giants have a winning or losing record on Monday Night Football?

4. Which Giants great has co-authored a range of children's books including titles called 'By My Brother's Side' and 'End Zone'?

5. In 1973 and 1974 the Giants played home games at which Connecticut stadium?

6. Of Giants quarterbacks with over 1,000 attempts, who has the lowest interception percentage?

7. Who was the only Giant to be a member of both the 1990 and 2000 Super Bowl rosters?

8. The Giants have defeated which opponent the most times in playoff games in team history?

9. In 2016, which Giant was the co-winner of the NFL Walter Payton Man of the Year Award alongside Arizona's Larry Fitzgerald?

10. True or false – The Giants have had at least one player selected to the Pro Bowl every year since 1986?

11. The Giants gifted a win to which rival thanks to the play known as 'The Miracle at the Meadowlands'?

12. Of Giants kickers with over 50 field goal attempts, who has the best conversion percentage?

13. You have to go back to 1997 to find the last tied game involving the Giants. Who were their opponents in that 7-7 ball game?

14. True or false – Odell Beckham Jr. holds the NFL record for the most catches by a rookie?

15. Joe Montana was knocked out during a 1986 playoff game against the Giants after a brutal hit from which lineman?

16. The Giants took part in the first ever NFL regular season game in London against which team?

17. What was the score in that game?

18. Which famous stadium hosted that historic match up?

19. What was the unofficial name of the 1950s-era team's dominant defense? a) Bowler Hat Defense b) Broom Defense c) Umbrella Defense

20. What is the highest number of points allowed by the Giants in a single season? a) 501 b) 511 c) 521

Quiz 12: Answers

1. Denver 2. 39-20 3. Rose Bowl 4. Phil Simms 5. Ottis (OJ) Anderson and Joe Morris 6. Zeke Mowatt, Mark Bavaro and Phil McConkey 7. Bill Parcells 8. Joe Morris 9. Bill Belichick 10. 14-2 11. Dallas and Seattle 12. Washington 13. San Francisco 14. True 15. Mark Bavaro 16. The Big Blue Wrecking Crew 17. Green Bay 18. Romeo Crennel 19. c) 30 20. c) Leonard Marshall

Quiz 14: 1990 World Champions

1. Which team did the Giants face in Super Bowl XXV?

2. What was the final score?

3. Which opposition kicker missed a 47-yard field goal with four seconds remaining to give the Giants the win?

4. Which head coach steered the team to their second Super Bowl triumph?

5. Which future Giants head coach was the team's receivers coach in 1990?

6. Who was the only Giant to catch a touchdown pass in Super Bowl XXV?

7. Which venue hosted Super Bowl XXV?

8. True or false – In Super Bowl XXV the Giants possessed the ball for over 40 minutes?

9. Which team did the Giants defeat 31-3 in the Divisional round of the playoffs?

10. The Giants reached Super Bowl XXV after defeating which team in the Conference Championship Game?

11. How many games did the Giants win in the 1990 regular season?

12. Which former New England head coach was the Giants offensive coordinator in 1990?

13. With 784 yards and 11 touchdowns, who was New York's leading rusher in 1990?

14. True or false – The Giants led the NFL allowing the fewest points in 1990?

15. Which lineman was the only Giants offensive player elected to the Pro Bowl that season?

16. Who kicked a 21-yard field goal late in the fourth quarter to give the Giants the lead in Super Bowl XXV?

17. Which long-time Dallas Cowboys cornerback led the Giants in interceptions in 1990, picking off six passes?

18. What was the only AFC opponent to beat the Giants during 1990?

19. How many points did the Giants offense score in the 1990 regular season? a) 315 b) 325 c) 335

20. The Giants started the 1990 season by winning how many straight games? a) 9 b) 10 c) 11

Quiz 13: Answers

1. 1925 2. Minnesota 3. Losing 4. Tiki Barber 5. Yale Bowl 6. Kerry Collins with 2.8% 7. Howard Cross 8. San Francisco 9. Eli Manning 10. False 11. Philadelphia 12. Josh Brown 13. Washington 14. False 15. Jim Burt 16. Miami 17. Giants 13-10 Dolphins 18. Wembley Stadium 19. c) Umbrella Defense 20. c) 501

Quiz 15: Pot Luck

1. Which running back set a franchise record after catching 13 passes against Dallas in January 2000?

2. Who was the Giants' general manager from 1979 through to 1997?

3. Which extremely tough Giant played five games during the 1986 season despite suffering from a fractured jaw?

4. In 2005, the Giants became only the fifth team in NFL history to have five players score seven or more touchdowns. Who were the famous five?

5. Since the 1970 AFL/NFL merger, who is the Giants' longest tenured head coach?

6. During the 1986 season the Giants wore a spider patch on their uniforms to honor which former defensive star who died of cancer that year?

7. True or false – The 2011 World Championship Giants had a negative regular season points differential?

8. Up to the start of the 2018 season the Giants had lost a team record five playoff games apiece to which two NFC teams?

9. Which trio of 2008 running backs were known as 'Earth, Wind and Fire'?

10. True or false – Odell Beckham Jr. was the first player in NFL history to catch over 80 passes for over 1,000 yards in each of his first three NFL seasons?

11. Which opposition quarterback never played again after breaking his leg following a Lawrence Taylor tackle in a November 1985 game?

12. The 2003 Giants endured a disastrous end to the season, losing how many games in a row?

13. True or false – Eli Manning threw at least 10 interceptions every year while with the Giants?

14. Pat Shurmur was the head coach of which AFC team in 2011 and 2012?

15. True or false - In the 1940s, the Giants wore red home jerseys?

16. The Giants defeated which AFC West opponent 28-7 in their 1,000th game in 1998?

17. Which former tight end is the sideline reporter on Giants radio broadcasts?

18. Which offensive lineman was the only starter on the Giants' Super Bowl XLII team whose first name and surname started with the same letter?

19. What color is the stripe that runs down the middle of the Giants helmet? a) gray b) red c) white

20. What is the highest number of sacks the Giants have recorded in a single season? a) 66 b) 67 c) 68

Quiz 14: Answers

1. Buffalo 2. 20-19 3. Scott Norwood 4. Bill Parcells 5. Tom Coughlin 6. Stephen Baker 7. Tampa Stadium 8. True 9. Chicago 10. San Francisco 11. 13 games 12. Ron Erhardt 13. Ottis (OJ) Anderson 14. True 15. Bart Oates 16. Matt Bahr 17. Everson Walls 18. Buffalo in week 14 19. c) 335 points 20. b) 10

Quiz 16: 2007 World Champions

1. Which team did the Giants face in Super Bowl XLII?

2. What was the score in the game?

3. Super Bowl XLII was hosted in which stadium?

4. True or false – New York's opening drive lasted nine minutes 59 seconds?

5. Who caught an amazing, one-handed, 32-yard pass on the final game-winning drive?

6. Who was named the MVP of Super Bowl XLII?

7. Which head coach masterminded the Super Bowl XLII triumph?

8. Who was the team's offensive coordinator in 2007?

9. Who was the team's defensive coordinator in 2007?

10. Which team did the Giants defeat in the Wild Card game?

11. The Giants defeated which rival 21-17 in the Divisional round playoff game?

12. The Giants reached Super Bowl XLII after defeating which team in the NFC Championship game?

13. True or false – The Giants were 12.5-point underdogs heading into Super Bowl XLII?

14. What was the team's 2007 regular season record?

15. With 1,009 yards who was the Giants' leading rusher in 2007?

16. Amazingly, only one member of the 2007 team received Pro Bowl honors. Which one?

17. True or false – The Giants lost their first two regular season games in 2007?

18. Which two Giants recorded double-digit sacks during the 2007 regular season?

19. Who was the referee in Super Bowl XLII? a) Mike Carey b) Ed Hochuli c) Bill Vinovich

20. Which musician headlined the half-time show at Super Bowl XLII? a) Mick Jagger b) Tom Petty c) Bruce Springsteen

Quiz 15: Answers

1. Tiki Barber 2. George Young 3. Mark Bavaro 4. Barber, Shockey, Burress, Toomer and Jacobs 5. Tom Coughlin 6. Carl Lockhart 7. True 8. Chicago and Green Bay 9. Brandon Jacobs, Derrick Ward and Ahmad Bradshaw 10. True 11. Joe Theismann 12. Eight 13. False – he threw 9 in 2004 14. Cleveland 15. True 16. Kansas City 17. Howard Cross 18. David Diehl 19. b) Red 20. c) 68

Quiz 17: Pot Luck

1. Which former Giant co-wrote a book called 'Sunday Morning Quarterback: Going Deep on the Strategies, Myths, and Mayhem of Football'?

2. What number jersey is worn by defender Jason Pierre-Paul?

3. In 2001, the Giants uniform featured a patch bearing the initials GBY to honor which long-time executive?

4. True or false – Eli Manning and Odell Beckham Jr. both attended the same Louisiana high school?

5. Which former defensive lineman's post-football career has included spells as a movie actor, singer, preacher and bodyguard for the Kennedy family?

6. Which four-time Pro Bowl punter was inducted into the Giants Ring of Honor in 2011?

7. Before Tom Coughlin, who was the last Giants head coach to have an overall winning record?

8. Who had more quarterback sacks while with the Giants – Justin Tuck or Osi Umenyiora?

9. Which Giants defensive great shares the same name as the record producer known as 'The Fifth Beatle'?

10. True or false – The official legal name of the team is the New York Football Giants?

11. What did the letter Y in the name of Y.A. Tittle stand for?

12. Up to the start of the 2018 season the Giants had a 100% losing record in playoff games against which two NFC teams?

13. True or false – Bill Parcells and Tom Coughlin have an identical 8-3 win loss playoff record with the Giants?

14. Defensive great Michael Strahan wore what number jersey?

15. What is the most times that the Giants have punted in a single regular season game?

16. What color jerseys did the Giants wear in Super Bowl XXV?

17. True or false – The Giants have a winning record against all of their NFC opponents?

18. Of all the teams currently in the NFL, which opponent have the Giants defeated the fewest times? (clue – it's an AFC team)

19. What was the seating capacity of the old Giants stadium? a) 80,242 b) 82,420 c) 84,202

20. What is the most interceptions thrown by Eli Manning in a single regular season? a) 25 b) 26 c) 27

Quiz 16: Answers

1. New England 2. Giants 17-14 Patriots 3. University of Phoenix Stadium 4. True 5. David Tyree 6. Eli Manning 7. Tom Coughlin 8. Kevin Gilbride 9. Steve Spagnuolo 10. Tampa Bay 11. Dallas 12. Green Bay 13. True 14. 10-6 15. Brandon Jacobs 16. Osi Umenyiora 17. True 18. Osi Umenyiora and Justin Tuck 19. a) Mike Carey 20. b) Tom Petty

Quiz 18: 2011 World Champions

1. Which team did the Giants face in Super Bowl XLVI?

2. What was the score in the game?

3. Who was named the game's Most Valuable Player?

4. Which stadium hosted Super Bowl XLVI?

5. Who was the only Giant to catch a touchdown pass in Super Bowl XLVI?

6. Whose 6-yard touchdown rush with less than a minute left proved to be the winning score of Super Bowl XLVI?

7. Which American Idol star sang the national anthem at Super Bowl XLVI?

8. Who was the defensive coordinator on the 2011 World Championship-winning team?

9. Who was the team's offensive coordinator in 2011?

10. Which team did the Giants defeat in the Wild Card round of the playoffs?

11. The Giants defeated which team 37-20 in the Divisional Round playoff?

12. The Giants reached Super Bowl XLVI after edging past which team 20-17 in the NFC Championship game?

13. The Giants secured the division title after coming out on top in a winner-take-all game against which rival?

14. Ahmad Bradshaw was one of two New York backs to rush for over 500 yards in 2011. Who was the other?

15. For the first time in team history the 2011 Giants had two receivers with over 1,000 receiving yards. Which two?

16. Which linebacker outmuscled Rob Gronkowski to record the only interception of Super Bowl XLVI?

17. Which two members of the 2011 roster were named in that season's NFC Pro Bowl team?

18. True or false – The 2011 Giants were the first team with a 9-7 regular season record to win the Super Bowl?

19. Who led the team in touchdowns in the 2011 regular season? a) Ahmad Bradshaw b) Victor Cruz c) Hakeem Nicks

20. The Giants lost how many straight games during the middle of the regular season? a) three b) four c) five

Quiz 17: Answers

1. Phil Simms 2. #90 3. George Young 4. True 5. Rosey Grier 6. Dave Jennings 7. Jim Fassel 8. Osi Umenyiora 9. George Martin 10. True 11. Yelberton 12. Carolina and Detroit 13. True 14. #92 15. 16 times 16. Blue 17. False 18. Baltimore 19. a) 80,242 20. c) 27

43

Quiz 19: Pot Luck

1. Who was the only member of the 2017 Giants team to receive Pro Bowl honors?

2. Who was the interim head coach for the final four games of the 2017 season?

3. Who is the only opposition quarterback to throw for over 300 yards against the Giants in a Super Bowl?

4. Who was the Giants starting center on their 1986 and 1990 World Championship-winning teams?

5. The 1993 Giants were eliminated in the Divisional round of the playoffs after being routed 44-3 by which team?

6. Which kicker, who was inducted into the Pro Football Hall of Fame in 2017, spent a single season with the Giants in 2001?

7. Which two former Giants defensive stars are the co-hosts of a weekly NFL TV show for the BBC in London?

8. True or false – The World Champion 2007 Giants had a regular season losing points differential?

9. In 2014, Odell Beckham Jr. became only the second player in NFL history with 90 or more receiving yards in nine straight games. Who, in 1995, was the first?

10. Who are the two Giants head coaches to lead the team to 11 wins in their debut season?

11. Who holds the team record for the most sacks in playoff games?

12. Which team routed the Giants by a score of 41-9 in their final game at Giants Stadium?

44

13. True or false – The 1994 FIFA World Cup Final was hosted at Giants Stadium?

14. Who was appointed the team's general manager in 2007?

15. Which Giant holds the record for the longest field goal in playoff games at Lambeau Field?

16. Who holds the franchise record for the most touchdowns by a rookie tight end?

17. True or false – The 2007 Giants were the first World Champions to win three road playoff games en route to the Super Bowl?

18. Who were the two offensive starters on the Super Bowl XLVI team whose first name and surname started with the same letter?

19. Which superstar headlined the half-time show at Super Bowl XLVI? a) Beyonce b) Janet Jackson c) Madonna

20. In what year did the Giants draft quarterback Phil Simms? a) 1978 b) 1979 c) 1980

Quiz 18: Answers

1. New England 2. Giants 21-17 Patriots 3. Eli Manning 4. Lucas Oil Stadium 5. Victor Cruz 6. Ahmad Bradshaw 7. Kelly Clarkson 8. Perry Fewell 9. Kevin Gilbride 10. Atlanta 11. Green Bay 12. San Francisco 13. Dallas 14. Brandon Jacobs 15. Victor Cruz and Hakeem Nicks 16. Chase Blackburn 17. Eli Manning and Jason Pierre Paul 18. True 19. a) Ahmad Bradshaw 20. b) Four

Quiz 20: Eli Manning

1. Eli Manning wears what number jersey?

2. In which Super Bowl-winning city was Eli born?

3. With which pick of the NFL Draft was Manning selected?

4. In what year did Eli make his regular season debut?

5. In what year was Eli born?

6. Eli made his regular season debut coming off the bench to replace which former Super Bowl-winning quarterback?

7. Which tight end caught Eli Manning's first career touchdown pass?

8. True or false – Eli has thrown at least two touchdown passes against the 31 other teams in the NFL?

9. How many games did Manning start in his rookie season?

10. Which receiver has caught more touchdown passes thrown by Eli than any other?

11. Eli is a shortened version of what full name?

12. Eli made his first regular season start against which NFC South team?

13. Manning is one of five players to win multiple Super Bowl MVP awards. Who are the other four?

14. True or false – Eli was a winner of the Heisman Trophy?

15. Three other quarterbacks were taken in the first round of the NFL Draft in which Eli was selected. Which three?

16. True or false – Eli has never thrown more picks than touchdowns in a single regular season?

17. What is the name of Eli's famous father?

18. On Christmas Eve 2017, Eli moved into sixth place in career passing yards, eclipsing which former AFC superstar?

19. In his first 14 seasons in the league Eli rushed for how many touchdowns? a) two b) four c) six

20. Up to the 2017 season, Eli had been voted to the Pro Bowl how many times? a) four b) five c) six

Quiz 19: Answers

1. Landon Collins 2. Steve Spagnuolo 3. John Elway 4. Bart Oates 5. San Francisco 6. Morten Andersen 7. Jason Bell and Osi Umenyiora 8. False 9. Michael Irvin 10. Dan Reeves and Ben McAdoo 11. Michael Strahan 12. Carolina 13. False 14. Jerry Reese 15. Lawrence Tynes 16. Evan Engram 17. False 18. David Diehl and Henry Hynoski 19. c) Madonna 20. b) 1979

Quiz 21: Pot Luck

1. Before taking the reins in New York, Tom Coughlin spent eight seasons as the head coach of which team?

2. In December 1982, which Giants head coach resigned to take charge of the Alabama Crimson Tide?

3. Which defensive lineman's three fumble-return touchdowns are the most in team history?

4. Which Giants great has appeared in a number of TV shows including 'Knight Rider', 'Orange Is The New Black' and 'The Electric Company'?

5. Before Odell Beckham Jr. in 2016, who was the last non-kicker to lead the team in scoring? (clue – it was in 1992)

6. The Giants blew a nine-point lead in the final two minutes of the 1997 Wild Card game to lose 23-22 to which team?

7. Which future Super Bowl-winning head coach was the Giants' offensive coordinator between 2000 and 2002?

8. In the 2011 playoffs, Eli Manning threw how many touchdown passes?

9. What is the longest field goal made by a Giants kicker in a Super Bowl?

10. True or false – The Giants have never hosted a home game on Thanksgiving?

11. Which former Giant is the host of the ABC TV gameshow 'The $100,000 Pyramid'?

12. True or false – Between 2005 and 2013 the Giants won eight straight overtime games?

13. The 2004 Giants wore a #79 sticker on their helmets in honor of which former player and coach?

14. Between 1996 and 2010 the Giants hosted their training camp at which educational establishment?

15. Which defensive star was the sole captain of the 1986 World Championship team?

16. What color uniform did the Giants wear in their Color Rush game in 2017?

17. Who was the Giants general manager from 1998 through to 2007?

18. What was the highest number of games lost by the Giants in a single season while Bill Parcells was head coach?

19. How much did MetLife Stadium cost to build? a) $1.4 billion b) $1.5 billion c) $1.6 billion

20. Between 2007 and 2012 kicker Lawrence Tynes converted how many straight extra points? a) 202 b) 204 c) 206

Quiz 20: Answers

1. #10 2. New Orleans 3. First 4. 2004 5. 1981 6. Kurt Warner 7. Jeremy Shockey 8. True 9. Seven 10. Odell Beckham Jr. 11. Elisha 12. Atlanta 13. Terry Bradshaw, Tom Brady, Joe Montana and Bart Starr 14. False 15. Philip Rivers, Ben Roethlisberger and JP Losman 16. False 17. Archie 18. John Elway 19. c) Six 20. a) Four

Quiz 22: History

1. The Giants played their first home game in franchise history at which famous stadium?

2. The Giants won the 1934 NFL Championship, defeating which opponent in the so-called 'Sneakers Game'?

3. In 1936, Art Lewis became a notable name in team history. Why?

4. True or false – The Giants were the first team to win the NFL Championship more than once?

5. Which quarterback, whose first name and surname start with the same letter, led the Giants to 57 wins between 1948 and 1961?

6. True or false – During World War II the Giants temporarily merged with the Eagles?

7. Which future Hall of Fame coach, who usually played in the secondary, started one game at quarterback in 1952?

8. Which versatile Giant finished in the top 10 in the NFL in rushing and receiving in 1957 and also threw two touchdown passes?

9. Which team defeated the Giants 23-17 in the 1958 NFL Championship, a contest dubbed 'The Greatest Game Ever Played'?

10. Between 1958 and 1963 the Giants lost in the NFL Championship game how many times?

11. What was added to the Giants helmet for the first time in 1961?

12. Which Giants quarterback was the winner of the AP NFL Most Valuable Player Award in 1962?

13. In 1967 the Giants sent four draft picks to the Vikings to acquire the services of which quarterback?

14. How many times did the Giants make the playoffs during the 1980s?

15. Which legendary tackle went to the Pro Bowl nine times between 1955 and 1965?

16. In what year did the Giants play their first game at Giants Stadium?

17. 'Prince Valiant' was a nickname of which Giants quarterback?

18. Which two Giants quarterbacks received Pro Bowl honors during the 1970s?

19. How many times did the Giants post a winning record during the 1970s? a) once b) twice c) three times

20. Tuffy Leamans was the first Giant to lead the NFL in which category? a) rushing b) receiving c) passing

Quiz 21: Answers

1. Jacksonville 2. Ray Perkins 3. Osi Umenyiora 4. Tiki Barber 5. Rodney Hampton 6. Minnesota 7. Sean Payton 8. Nine 9. 38 yards 10. True 11. Michael Strahan 12. True 13. Rosey Brown 14. University at Albany 15. Harry Carson 16. White 17. Ernie Accorsi 18. 12 19. c) $1.6 billion 20. b) 204

Quiz 23: Pot Luck

1. Which fearsome defensive lineman authored a book called 'Needlepoint For Men'?

2. Which versatile Giant went to the Pro Bowl eight times between 1953 and 1963 as a defensive back, running back and receiver?

3. The #7 jersey is retired in honor of which legendary offensive lineman?

4. Odell Beckham Jr. played college ball at which school?

5. With 153 victories between 1930 and 1953 which head coach has the most wins in franchise history?

6. The 2002 Giants lost the Wild Card game to which opponent after blowing a team-record 24-point lead?

7. Which Giants defender was the first African-American inducted into the Pro Football Hall of Fame?

8. Before becoming a head coach in the NFL Tom Coughlin spent three seasons in charge of which college program?

9. True or false – The Giants didn't defeat a single NFC opponent during the 2017 season?

10. True or false - The defending Super Bowl champions started the 1987 season by dropping five straight games?

11. In 1991, who became the just the fourth running back in team history to enjoy a 1,000-yard rushing season?

12. Between 2013 and 2016, Giants head coach Pat Shurmur was the offensive coordinator at which NFC East rival?

13. Which two teams appeared in the first Super Bowl hosted at MetLife Stadium?

14. Who was the first Giants receiver to catch 12 passes in a game more than once in his rookie season?

15. True or false – The Giants haven't scored an offensive touchdown on Thanksgiving Day since 1938?

16. What was the most games lost by the Giants in a single season while Tom Coughlin was head coach?

17. Tiki Barber was just the third player in NFL history to gain 10,000 rushing and 5,000 receiving yards. Who were the first two?

18. Who is the only Giant to record four or more sacks in a single game more than once?

19. What was the given name of former star linebacker Pepper Johnson? a) Daniel b) Joseph c) Thomas

20. What is the most points that the Giants have scored in a single regular season? a) 428 b) 438 c) 448

Quiz 22: Answers

1. The Polo Grounds 2. Chicago Bears 3. He was the team's first ever draft pick 4. True 5. Charlie Conerly 6. False 7. Tom Landry 8. Frank Gifford 9. Baltimore Colts 10. Five times 11. The NY logo 12. Y.A. Tittle 13. Fran Tarkenton 14. Five time 15. Rosey Brown 16. 1976 17. Phil Simms 18. Fran Tarkenton and Norm Snead 19. b) Twice 20. a) Rushing

Quiz 24: Anagrams

Rearrange the letters to make the name of a current or former Giants player or coach.

1. Gin Lineman

2. Might Uncool

3. Terry Allowance

4. Yardmen Photon

5. Crab Spell Ill

6. Rips Sox Curable

7. Ranch Rosary

8. Main Tearoom

9. Mini You Arose

10. Unjust Tick

11. Newest Larceny

12. Snarl Back

13. Rabbi I Trek

14. Calls In London

15. Ay Diverted

16. Paper Journalise

17. Bravo Karma

18. Trades Notions

19. Flee Jets Froth

20. Hens Cries

Quiz 23: Answers

1. Rosey Grier 2. Frank Gifford 3. Mel Hein 4. Louisiana State 5. Steve Owen 6. San Francisco 7. Emlen Tunnell 8. Boston College 9. False 10. True 11. Rodney Hampton 12. Philadelphia 13. Seattle and Denver 14. Odell Beckham Jr. 15. True 16. Ten 17. Marcus Allen and Marshall Faulk 18. Lawrence Taylor 19. c) Thomas 20. c) 448

Quiz 25: Numbers Game

Name the jersey number that was worn by the following players

1. Joe Morris and Prince Amukamara

2. Odell Beckham Jr. and Kurt Warner

3. Victor Cruz and Jeremy Shockey

4. Rodney Hampton and Brandon Jacobs

5. Pete Gogolak and Brad Daluiso

6. Steve Smith and Scott Brunner

7. Jason Sehorn and Aaron Ross

8. Pepper Johnson and Jonathan Casillas

9. Kerry Collins and Sean Landeta

10. Jumbo Elliott and Chris Snee

11. Lawrence Tynes and Brad Wing

12. Tiki Barber and Landon Collins

13. Mark Bavaro and Kevin Boss

14. Justin Tuck and Robert Ayers

15. Plaxico Burress and Dave Brown

16. Carl Banks and Antonio Pierce

17. Osi Umenyiora and Doug Riesenberg

18. Ahmad Bradshaw and Maurice Carthon

19. Jeff Hostetler and Craig Morton

20. Andy Robustelli and Amani Toomer

Quiz 24: Answers

1. Eli Manning 2. Tom Coughlin 3. Lawrence Taylor 4. Rodney Hampton 5. Bill Parcells 6. Plaxico Burress 7. Harry Carson 8. Amani Toomer 9. Osi Umenyiora 10. Justin Tuck 11. Lawrence Tynes 12. Carl Banks 13. Tiki Barber 14. Landon Collins 15. David Tyree 16. Jason Pierre-Paul 17. Mark Bavaro 18. Ottis Anderson 19. Jeff Hostetler 20. Chris Snee

Printed in Great Britain
by Amazon